X

MARKS

THE

DRESS

X
MARKS
THE
DRESS

A REGISTRY

KRISTINA MARIE DARLING
&
CAROL GUESS

A Karen & Michael Braziller Book
PERSEA BOOKS / NEW YORK

Thank you to the following magazines, in which
early versions of these poems first appeared:
Barn Owl Review, elimae, Rufous City Review, Stone Highway Review

The authors would both like to express their gratitude to
Jared Michael Wahlgren of Gold Wake Press.

Persea Books, Inc.
90 Broad Street
New York, NY 10004

Library of Congress Cataloging-in-Publication Data

Names: Darling, Kristina Marie, author. | Guess, Carol, 196– author.
Title: X marks the dress : a registry / Kristina Marie Darling & Carol Guess.
Description: Second edition. | New York : Persea Books, [2022] | "A Karen & Michael
Braziller book." | Summary: "An innovative queering of some of the most recognizable
conventions of heteronormative matrimony"—Provided by publisher.
Identifiers: LCCN 2021051261 | ISBN 9780892555475 (paperback ; acid-free paper)
Subjects: LCGFT: Poetry.
Classification: LCC PS3604.A746 X2 2022 | DDC 811/.6—dc23/eng/20211021
LC record available at https://lccn.loc.gov/2021051261

Second edition
Book design and composition by Rita Lascaro
Typeset in Adobe Caslon

Manufactured in the United States of America.
Printed on acid-free paper.

CONTENTS

X

MARKS

THE

DRESS

3-TIERED STEAMER

My pink comes from before. Your house breathes faster. Tonight I'll break your heart and leave you street corner easy: besotted, best beast. I pick you up at 8, a little late for a Coke and a candy apple. Your father waves you off, but he's misplaced your mother, so she comes, too: curled in the backseat, chignon nonplussed. You've brought your favorite dimestore purse, pleather and calico. Pink is learning. The vulgar present is calling. I pull you inside out.

{Pierced Tablespoons}

Your music begins after. Finally the room holds
still. Now I'll open my dresser drawer & find the
gifts you've left behind: torn gloves, a dirty glass,
some flowers pressed in a book. I place each one of
them on a mahogany shelf, record their height in a
tiny ledger. You've given me enough trinkets for a
museum, but I hear the same bells ringing. Soon
there's nothing but music, a white strap slipping
from my shoulder. It's like you never left.

Strapless, you slip into the suicide seat. We swipe
bicyclists and barn doors barreling detours. The
highway knows which way to turn. Forked road,
forks, and a flask for a picnic. I read to you from a
cereal box. Here's plastic sushi and candied lemon,
fallen apples and dandelion tea. Your hair covers your
eyes. You twist statements to questions. Confession:
I've never kept orchids alive. Down Main Street,
mannequins proffer bouquets: carnations, stitched.
Your duct-taped lips.

{CUPS & SAUCERS}

My tea stains came from your picnic. Now the kettle boils & shrieks. Tomorrow you'll fasten your diamond cufflinks & leave me disheveled, waiting: torn dress, wilted corsage, clutching a few dollars for a cab. When I open the door I feel a little old for a trinket or flowers pressed in a book. But I should warn you: there are always mementos, & I've only begun my collection. Before long I'll enshrine you on a red satin pillow. I'll display your former self in a glass cabinet.

CROCHETED TISSUE BOX HOLDER

Sometimes things go wrong at weddings. Someone
steps on the veil or loses the ring. In a "trash the
dress" photo on the bank of a river, one bride lost
her footing, dead weight in her dress. I can't save
you; I can only be careful. For example, my mistress
won't help with the cake. For example, we won't get
married in Texas, where I'm wanted for something
I'll never confess. Don't worry your pretty neck over
dresses: tea-colored silk, Rosaline lace. We'll lash
our rings to a red satin pillow. Keep the flower girl
leashed. Use erasable ink.

{CHAMPAGNE FLUTES}

After the toast, my search for you began. Beneath dirty tablecloths & cracked plates. My white dress torn from celebration after celebration. Tonight you'll reappear, disheveled, yet ready: black tuxedo, mud-stained shoes, your outstretched hand waiting. But I can't decide between the liquors and the desserts, a candy bride nestled at the top of the heap. Before long you'll fasten me to a satin pillow. I'll see my car keys locked in your kitchen cabinet.

His-and-Hers Key Rings

Who stole your keys? I don't mind your crooked driving. We're parked for the night. It's only our wedding, night to mark each other mine, twin halves of a mortgage or the company car. Off with the dress. I unstrangle your garter, twist off the ring I bartered last month. I'll have you ringless and drunk. Nostalgia begins at home, in a sea of tulle, my cummerbund coiled in a corner to strike. You're prettiest when you're on top. I'll prop you up and promise to ask for directions if I'm ever lost.

{Ice Bucket}

There are so many things that can go wrong in a marriage. Most nights I can't decide between our mortgage & a getaway car. Soon I'll disappear again, a sea of tulle swallowed in a Coup de Ville: torn lace, broken stilettos, your pale hand waving from the side of the street. But you still won't choose between your bride & the mistress. Tomorrow she'll phone you from the backseat of a cab, ringless, drunk on mimosa. She's at her best when she's helpless. I'm prettiest in a wedding album, every ruffle on my dress neatly pressed, every strand of my hair in place.

GIFT CERTIFICATE TO VICTORIA'S SECRET

Mother was a runaway bride, handkerchief waving from the back of a train. Met my father in the Five-and-Dime, or so she says on Monday and Tuesday. On Wednesday she says I was stolen, not birthed. On Thursday, no talking. Weekends are for orphans. I'm so many men in the back of a cab. Husband or lover? Plastic or paper? Sometimes I'm a woman, too: stiletto heels and a blue silk bra. I practice walking twice a day. The lingerie you found is mine.

Lately even the furniture keeps secrets. Behind
the divan I find high-heeled shoes, lingerie, a pink
lace handkerchief. Your other life stashed between
cracks in the sofa. So maybe I'm the one who should
be waving goodbye from the back of a train. Before,
as church bells sounded, I could hear my mother
cheering. The bridesmaids clawing for one bouquet.
That was when the room held still. But these nights
I'm a woman too: lipstick, blue silk, an easy-bake
oven ready to smolder.

SPRINGFORM CAKE PAN

I've never seen you burn. Your cakes slide out of the oven iced. I've never seen you break a glass or heel or heart, unless I count: half-heart, half-heel. Mornings, I put on my workday suit, but nothing's working. I walk to the deli. Fired months ago, I'm feral: white man in a suit with nowhere to go. My boss turns his back when I pass his window, six yards away or six feet deep. There are six of me, at least: two in lingerie, one dead, one busking dime bags off the bascule bridge. One's respectable, the one you kiss. And number six? Even I don't know his story. I married you hoping you'd tell me his name.

{ICE CREAM SCOOP}

You've never seen me burn, but who said ice can't be sweet? I'm still all cake knives & frosting, the fondant heaped on a silver platter. Nights I practice smoldering, but you're never impressed. You watch with your hair slicked, briefcase packed, a handkerchief folded in your front pocket. Fired from the used car lot, you've been looking for something to work at. But I'm such a slow learner, the ice on my dress never seems to thaw: pale hands, cold silk, every ribbon frozen in place.

How do you sever a lie from the life it's leading? I'm tired of pretending to test drive cars. Pretending's a job, tang of snake oil underneath my tongue. Our health insurance runs out in two weeks. You can't get sick, can't see a dentist, can't look at the world through rose-colored glasses because glasses, Sweetheart, cost the sky. We'll manage catastrophic for a while, but first I have to sit you down, carve a wife from a block of ice. I'm tired of boxers and motor oil. While you're off shopping I change into my favorite dress and sway to love songs in our bedroom mirror. The woman I am would tell you the truth.

[Wedding Favor: Heart-shaped Bird Seed Cake]

Rice expands, explodes, and kills, feathering the bride's lace dress. Compassionate or urban myth? Whatev. I know too much to say I do: the way you walk in flirty skirts, the knots you beg for, bending over. You asked me first; I'm not that girl. Three years later you're an invitation. I crocheted a tissue holder, pink the slip you hide inside. You'll introduce me as Adele, name you go by in my unlit room. I smell suburbs on her breath. I love you more because I love you both.

{PULL-OUT CLOSET ORGANIZER & SHOE RACK}

Since when is pretending a job? I'm still paying the mortgage with my fashion sense: pink sunglasses, matching pumps, & your favorite dress. Nights like this I walk the boulevard, asking for a handout. Men will offer me rides & fine chocolate as you watch from the kitchen window. Stilettoed & frostbitten, I keep looking for someone to warm me up. I've been such an unruffled bride that the lace on my skirt is starting to unravel. Clothes cost money, darling. A husband like you should foot the bill.

[WEDDING FAVOR: SOAP BUBBLES]

Tiny silver soap burst mirrors surround the happy
couple: cake toppers drowning in fondant. But why
only two figurines on the cake? Aren't there three of
us, layered and endless? Or four, if I count Adele—
your other, best self. We met online, girls seeking
girls. You kept your secret until we sat at the bar,
strangers seeking each other in others. I looked
right through you until you said my name. Made
the cabbie serpentine the sleeping city in case you
stalked me. But curiosity's my better half, and half
of you attracts me. She's beautiful, your bridled wife.
I've asked to meet her once too often. Tonight she
shimmers, silver ring blown high enough to burst.

My father the jeweler kept a dog on watch, coal-eyed shepherd carved from stone. Nights, he undraped faceless necks. Queer combinations kept his diamonds locked. The thief that bilked him wore a ruffled dress, a pout like yours, a loaded gun. Sweetheart, the parts of me you want aren't mine. The woman I'm not is realer than the man I only seem to be. Your wrists deserve sapphires, not manacles—sorry. Some necklaces are strangers' candy.

[Wedding Favor: Chocolate Truffles]

She drops a penny on the stoop, spun copper truffle. I've never been inside your house, but now I've knocked, and now I'm in. She wrote me such a charming thanks—pink scented paper, chocolate ink. I wrote back, and she wrote too, and here we are, so anti-Google. We're sitting down to tea, no joke. She talks about lipstick and she talks about church. After mimosas she starts on you. Albert, I say. She calls you Bert. I want to scream your name—Adele—but after A I'm staring at her perfect mouth, still mouthing worlds. Clavicle. Delicious. Eat.

{SILVER PLATTER}

Who gave you jewelry? I've been cleaning the kitchen cabinets in my Sunday best: pencil skirt, black leather boots, & just enough perfume. Nights I dress for a different kind of domestication. But she's left you cold as sheet metal, a loaded gun in someone else's fireproof box. This morning she dropped you on the front lawn, all concrete & steel, but the combination you gave me stopped working. Now you're fingering the clasp on her necklace, its tiny lock & key. I'll need more than just a blowtorch, or a little dial set to "high heat."

Who uses a blowtorch to open a letter? Who's scrubbing the kitchen in black leather boots? My wife wears rickrack and calico skirts; this creature's an interloper. Sweetheart, I still haven't told you: I'm Albert at dinner, Adele in the cube. My new job's transparent; hired in heels, I'm ready with six must-have separates for Spring. Mornings, I change in the bus station bathroom: Women's or Men's, wrong life out or in. I can't keep my two lives together much longer. Once the M on my license goes missing, our marriage dissolves: two women mean nothing.

[WEDDING FAVOR: COIN PURSE]

Your wife snaps the butterfly clasp on her purse. It's easy to ask when you know what you want. She's boy crazy, flirting with the teenager chained to our pizza. While she folds his tip I tiptoe upstairs. Your wedding bed kneels on arthritic haunches. Flip-flops off, I fall face first: ruffles and flounces, a violet divan. Who sleeps on so many decorative pillows? I'm tired of threeways where no one gets fucked. Downstairs, your wife's enjoying her pizza. Her crush drives off in a cheese-colored car.

{Water Goblets}

Your girlfriend licks sugar off the rim of a crystal
shot glass. What happens to the wedding gifts if a
marriage dissolves? Before, it was easy to send thank
you notes: white scented paper, matching envelopes,
& dark green ink. But now you're changing in the
bathroom, unbuttoning the shirt I bought for you at
some Labor Day sale. Soon I see you all pale blue
in someone else's designer dress. I've undone the
little clasp on my purse, searching for gift receipts.
Sweetheart, your new bride is waiting in her mud-
stained car. The husband I remember wouldn't look
back.

Flowers in my hair, white scarf, pink nails: no looking back as I board the ship. Catnapping on deck leaves creases in linen. I'll iron my skirt before cruising the bar. Here's endless water and a lidded sun; in three days we'll dock and I'll sign off on Albert. Overboard without a trace. I've changed my surname, as some women do. Here's salt on a glass the color of sunset, here's a toast to lost luggage and a one-way fare. History begins with the future, perfect. I re-apply lipstick behind door number 2.

[Wedding Favor: Votive Candle]

We carried wedding china through the woods
behind your house. Smashed each piece against
a tree. You asked again if I wanted a ticket, salt
over our shoulders on a seaside voyage. I said no
and I'll say it again. I love people in the strangest
ways. Besides, you set your house on fire. What
kind of lover wastes matches on wood? I've got two
cigarettes in my back pocket, and a quarter for the
jukebox in a bar downtown. Every stranger wants a
different song. At the end of your ocean is another
small town.

APPENDIX
A

Marginalia & Other Misc. Fragments

---

1. A rare variety of orchid, which was mounted and displayed on a silver placard.

2. She snipped the red flowers as the music began. Her fingers intertwined with the cold metal shears.

3. "I had wanted to free myself from the endless parade of feminine embellishments. Within every window the same bouquet of pink roses. Now a vase lies shattered at my feet."

†1. The quality of appearing real or true.
‡2. Something that only seems real or true (See also: the bride's alibi).

5. The autobiographical novel depicts a heroine's pursuit of an alternative to marriage, particularly the social conventions governing the ceremony itself. Although the manuscript was destroyed in a housefire, a preliminary sketch of the altar can be found in the library's special collections.

6. "It was only then I understood that I 'needed time.' My white dress torn from the endless celebrations. Behind each lace inlay I could feel the most fragile stitches holding it all in place."

7. *Effilé.* Translated from the French as "tenuous."

8. Meaning the bride's preparations for the elaborate ceremony. Her silver pendant held both the old photographs and a lock of tangled hair.

9. Compare, in this case, to an unruly garden.

ENDNOTES TO A HISTORY OF
WEDDING INVITATIONS

---

1. A hardened steel tool, most often used for engraving.

2. She sealed the envelope when the inscription was complete. The darkest flower blooming along the paper's scalloped edge.

3. "I had wanted to preserve the cream coloured note you gave to me that evening. But my chiffonier smolders and now the keepsake burning in a locked room."

4. *Correspond.*
    †1. To be in similar in origin, nature, or function.
    ‡2. To communicate by letter, usually for a period of time.

5. The documentary follows a woman through her fire-damaged house. The film itself indicates where she would have kept these champagne flutes and dead orchids.

6. "It was then I wished for an address where I could send this small memento. Within the box I had placed the most fragile statuette. Now the glass lies shattered at my feet."

7. *Courrier.* Translated from the French as "delivery."

8. She opened his letter when the shades were drawn. Even then she could barely decipher the Latin epigraph, its belaboured flourishes.

9. Meaning the bride's ruined dress. The white lace still bristling at her ankles.

---

bride. A woman who chooses her attire without anticipating its inevitable interpretation. In the wedding album, her shoulders are bare and visible above the lace trimmings on a white silk dress.

correspondence. Meaning the letters sent between guests of this lavish ceremony. Their exchange gave rise to a fascination with the bride's green earrings, their endless variety.

delivery. The envelope that appeared beneath her door that evening. Note its cream coloured paper and elaborate wax seal.

dress. To bedeck oneself or another. She had hoped the dark blue nightdress would entice but also threaten and trouble him. Its diaphanous sleeves and intricately embellished hemline.

epigraph. Meaning the belaboured quotation that appeared at the beginning of his note. She was reminded that an invitation, once made, cannot be unmade.

paper. In this case, tinder for the fire. She lit a makeshift wick as the light began to fade. The envelope's scalloped edge curling like petals on a dark flower.

ruined. The bride who charms without adhering to social conventions. For a more detailed explanation, see the attached appendix on feminine etiquette, the infinite possible missteps.

An Index of Illustrations

figure 1. This small armoire was said to house an elaborate collection of unused wedding invitations and matching cream-coloured envelopes.

figure 2. From a series of watercolours that attempt to render the interior of the bride's jewelry box. It had become commonplace to depict her fragile body as a small bird under lock and key.

figure 3. A lost photograph, which captured the groom as he boarded a luxury ocean liner. The artist would later lament the loss of this unnamed man at sea.

figure 4. A portrait of the bride, in which she is wearing both a silver pendant and a pair of green earrings with pearl inlays.

figure 5. A preliminary sketch, which depicts the wedding as a parade of memorable objects. Each of the groomsmen carried a small memento in his front pocket.

figure 6. The diagram displays various inconsistencies in the bride's emotions. Note the conflict between her obvious devotion and her desire to explore the burned house.

figure 7. The unworn garter, which was last seen billowing across a field of scorched grass and wilted flowers.

figure 8. A scene in which the guests' names are written in an enormous ledger. When she closed the book, they heard the most startling music.

2. She arranged her hair when the shade was drawn. The darkest
flowers bristling against her ears.

3. "I realized that a bride must choose not only between the
two men, but between herself and others. And now the most
fragile corsage tethered to my wrist."

4. *Restrain.*

    1. To hold back or prevent.
    †2. To deprive of freedom or liberty.
    ‡3. To restrict.

5. The documentary follows a woman from an engagement to her wedding ceremony. Upon showing the film, viewers were troubled by the prevalence of suicide in the work's numerous subplots.

6. She held the ring before the tiny window and watched it shimmer.

7. *Prise au piège.* Translated from the French as "entrapment."

8. "It was only then I realized I had chosen wrongly. The corsage has wilted and now his letters smolder in a locked room."

9. Note the tiny birds etched into each piece of their wedding china.

10. Compare, in its present state, to the burned house.

APPENDIX
B

Dictionary of Nuptial Slang

The baker had many cats. He believed that sick or aging cats thrived on icing; in particular, small icing sculptures shaped like mice. Occasionally he observed a particular friendship developing among the cats—a tabby believing it belonged with a Siamese, for example; or a long-haired feral smitten with a Russian Blue. When such friendships developed, he performed a wedding. The cake was made of catnip-scented cardboard. At the top of the cake he placed twin candy mice. The cats refused to eat the mice, preferring live mice that lived in the field.

CHIFFONIER

Before dinner the weather changed suddenly,
wind rushing across the scorched grass and wilted
flowers. We were cold, so we decided to burn the
chiffonier.

We didn't have an ax, but we had the pierced
tablespoons your uncle had given us. The pattern
was spiders spinning a web. The bowl of each
spoon was web-shaped. Although they were made
of recycled plastic and tended to melt, we cherished
them, keeping them in the jewelry box your sister
gave us.

We stabbed at the chiffonier, cutlery gnashing.
Our efforts warmed us, and we sat down to eat.

CHURCH

As a child, my father took me to different houses of worship. He wanted me to be open-minded, to respect the variety of human beliefs.

I tried very hard to feel God in each house. When the loudspeaker boomed I felt angry, worried that God had been speaking to me at just that moment and I'd missed out. I read signs in the absence of windows, in the chill of the freezer, in standing in line.

When my father was dying, he asked me to pray with him. I held his hand while he murmured something. It sounded like he was talking to a cereal box.

Later, while I adjusted his pillows, I asked him what his prayer meant.

"I was praying to a cereal box," he explained. "Food is sacred, so I worship in supermarkets."

All at once my childhood made sense.

The tabloid hymnals, the popsicle saints.

Decorative Pillows

When I'm having sex with a stranger in a hotel,
I try not to worry about the decorative pillows.
Instead I worry about the bedspread (which I
remove by wrapping my hand with the plastic
laundry bag), and the remote control (which
I cover with a plastic sandwich bag), and the
stranger. Once, after an especially gorgeous
encounter of mutual satisfaction, a particular
stranger asked me if she was still a stranger, having
just shared something so intimate. I asked for her
middle name and her favorite color. Both were
violet, which I found hard to believe.

I lived alone. I had lovers and friends and pets and projects. I kept my coffee pot warm, real cream in the fridge. I had trees and a garden, pressed flowers and photos. My sofa was soft and my mattress was firm.

It was a good life, but my friends and family never believed me. There's someone out there for you, they said.

This made me think of a moon-faced man pacing the streets, searching for my cheerful calico curtains, my well-stocked kitchen. The moon-faced man would smash my windows, undaunted by my growling dog.

In the morning I'd find him sitting at my pink formica table, eating buttered toast, reading a magazine fished from recycling.

Surprise! He'd say. I'm the one your friends and family were talking about. I'm here!

And I would live with this man for the rest of my life.

Green Earrings With Pearl Inlays

By the time I turned forty, I knew that I would never be married.

Not to a man.

Not to a woman.

Not to a poly play partner.

Not to a diety.

I knew that I would never be married because I didn't want to be married. I avoided marriage with the same passion with which others pursued it.

I did, however, want a pair of green earrings with pearl inlays.[1]

I invited friends and family to my non-wedding party, a non-ceremony during which I would not get married.

A few days later someone knocked on my door. A stranger stood on my stoop, arms full of packages. One of the wineglasses broke in the mail, but the green earrings sparkled when I pinned back my hair.

---

[1] Also, I wanted a four-speed juicer.

HEALTH INSURANCE

On my new job, I finally had health insurance.
Shortly after visiting a doctor, dentist, therapist,
and various specialists, I received a letter
explaining my deductible. My deductible was one
billion dollars.

I called the number at the bottom of the letter. An
automated voice asked me to punch in my social
security number, identification code, zip code,
and number of calories consumed daily (including
alcohol, but excluding "free foods"). Then the
automated voice began speaking in soothing tones.
It was a test to see if I could be hypnotized over the
phone. If I could be hypnotized, I would win.

When I emerged from what felt like a refreshing
catnap, it was winter and the yard was covered
in snow. I had lost my job and with it, my health
insurance. My prize was a penny in a Cracker Jack
box.

His-and-Hers

Everyone brought babies to the batchlorette
party. Some were real and some were fake. Some
were borrowed, and although none were blue,
at least one of the real live babies had been born
prematurely, and had lived for weeks in a tiny tent.
The mother of the tiny baby remembered keeping
vigil beside the tent; later, when her baby could
breathe and text on its own, she showed pictures
of its tiny footprint. The baby, now a teenager,
didn't believe her. After all, she had told the baby
teenager that the internet hadn't always existed,
and that she had been a man in a previous life.

Labor Day Sale

My best friend and I went dress shopping on Labor Day. She avoided old-fashioned shops with ruffled dresses and pastel bridesmaids' gowns, preferring places with names like "Wed."

After several near misses we tried a new store downtown. "Ball & Chain" had stained concrete floors. Salesgirls paced in black leather boots. Oxblood curtains hung to the floor.

At this shop they strapped metal balls to the ankle of the bride-to-be. There were different finishes to the metal. Some were shiny and some were matte; some had thick chains and some moved when she moved. It was difficult to choose between gold and silver chains, because my friend's ring was silver, but her earrings were gold.

LEDGER

Before Facebook, Twitter, texting, blogging, email, and everything else, the bride and groom each kept a ledger to record the details of their special day.

After the ceremony, the ledgers were smeared with flour and buried under the chicken coop.[2]

[2.] If the groom's family did not keep chickens, the bride was pilloried.

PIZZA

One night, when the kids were in bed and the house was quiet, we flipped through our wedding album. We teared up remembering our vows, and laughed at photos of our dog in the pool.

As we flipped through the album, I noticed a handsome stranger standing half in, half out of several photos. He seemed to belong at another wedding, as if he'd wandered into the wrong hotel.

How odd, I said, that a stranger ended up in so many of our photos. He's even in photos we took at home. Look, I said, he's petting our dog. He's cutting our cake. He's hugging your mom.

You twisted your ring. He's not a stranger.

Oh, I said. I tried to let it go.

A few minutes later I put down the album. Who is that man and what is he doing in our wedding photos?

Darling, you said, don't be angry.

I'm not angry, I said. Not yet.

Would you like me to order pizza?

No, I said. Explain that man.

Darling, you know how my mother and father rejected me? How they said they couldn't support our relationship, that our wedding was an insult to God? Well, I told my parents I was marrying a man. I hired an actor to play my husband. It was just so they'd come to our wedding. We put the cake in the other room.

I went into the kitchen and came back with a cup of coffee from the pot I'd made that morning.

Darling? I did the ceremony real quick, just a few people, my brother and your brother, too, and then everyone joined us for the party. I've been meaning to tell you. He has an apartment on the south side of town. I go there sometimes to have dinner with my parents. He has kids from his first marriage, Becky and Jeff.

Those are our kids' names.

I know, you said. That's why we had to name them Becky and Jeff.

I looked at the wedding album. We were dancing, dresses swirling. Our bridesmaids danced with us, a cluster of women. Your actor-husband was off to the side, frosting smeared on his face like paint.

Six Must-Have Separates For Spring

1. *Cream-colored linen skirt.* For swimming or drowning.

2. *White button-down shirt, three-quarter sleeves.* Edible buttons make this a practical purchase.

3. *Pale pink sweater, thin cotton.* May be used as a leash.

4. *Ivory slacks, low-rise.* This year's collection calls for legs to be stitched together at the inner seam.

5. *Blue silk sleeveless shell.* Includes ocean sound audio.

6. *One "fun" item, such as a scarf, belt, or handbag.* For burying the unwanted.

A few hours before my wedding I began to paint again, something I had once seen as a hobby. My new work reflected an awareness of art history, juxtaposed with an innate understanding of color, space, and design. Over the course of an hour I gained self-confidence and fully embraced my ambition, jettisoning my day job as a barista. I locked myself in an upper room and began painting in earnest. The first series avoided the use of white entirely, but my second (and still best-known) series incorporated shards of white fabric, over which I smeared gray, blue, and black lines, which stuttered into dots and dashes. Since then I have rarely emerged from my room, save for the occasional dedication of my work to a gallery or museum, or to buy candy necklaces for their sublime pastels.

Unworn Garter

She wanted to do things differently. Most brides wore white, so she wore blue. Most brides carried flowers, so she carried dead leaves. Most brides served cake, so she served beets.

She wanted her garter to be unique. After all, he would tug it down her thigh, in full view of their guests. They would know things she didn't know yet, and wouldn't know until much later.

She decided on a tattoo that looked exactly like a satin garter. When the time came he knelt and she lifted. He scraped at her thigh while she gritted her teeth.

Used Car Lot

One night, when the children were grown and had
cars of their own, we remembered believing that
cars could talk. We wanted to believe this so badly
that we came to believe it with certainty. Some
cars stuttered and some had accents; for example,
the Coup de Ville sounded British. At first,
cars parroted our speech, but then they became
more articulate about their own journeys, fuel,
and desires. Sometimes, when they spoke in low
voices at night, lights dim and the radio for cover,
we worried they might be plotting to overthrow
us. We envisioned being trapped in a car wash,
wearing almost nothing while warm, soapy water
slicked back our hair and headlights bound us in
their unwavering gaze.

APPENDIX
C

What Survived the Housefire

My pink   breathes faster.

          I pull from inside out.

Pierced

museum

                    you never left

Strapless, you slip

        from

             apples and dandelion tea.

shrieks

leave me disheveled

I should warn you

The veil ,   the ring,

dead weight.

I can't decide between
a candy bride

a glass cabinet

It's only

night.

The dress

begins   a sea. You're prettiest

when

you're   lost.

                                               between our

mortgage &

      broken stilettos

I was stolen.

stashed between

                    my mother
clawing

I've   only seen you iced.

                                        Nights I
practice

                        looking

                  frozen

A block of ice,

love songs.   I   would
tell you the truth.

Heart-shaped

suburbs.

I love you more.

Closet

ed

&   bitten, I keep looking

Silver   mirrors surround the

secret.

She's beautiful,   bridled.

ruffled dress, a pout   , a loaded gun.

inside your house,

a

perfect mouth,   mouthing worlds.

diamonds

fingering

a little dial

marriage

dissolves:

She's
chained

face first:

Your   friend licks

envelopes
        in the bathroom, unbuttoning

Flowers in my hair,

a linen   skirt

History begins

.

$$X^3$$

3. The guests could hear her dress rustling as she walked away from the altar. Even then, the white lace trim had begun to unravel.

ABOUT THE COLLABORATORS

KRISTINA MARIE DARLING

is the author of thirty-six books. Her work has been recognized with awards from Yaddo, the American Academy in Rome, Fundación Valparaíso, the Heinz Foundation, Cité Internationale des Arts in Paris; and the Whiting Foundation. Born and raised in the American Midwest, she now divides her time between the United States and Europe.

CAROL GUESS

is the author of twenty books of poetry and prose, including *Doll Studies: Forensics* and *Tinderbox Lawn*. Her short fiction collection *Sleep Tight Satellite* is forthcoming in 2023. A frequent collaborator, she writes across genres and illuminates historically marginalized material. In 2014 she was awarded the Philolexian Award for Distinguished Literary Achievement by Columbia University. She is Professor of English at Western Washington University, where she teaches Queer Studies and Creative Writing. She lives in Seattle.